The Pain You Caused

a book of poetry

NATASHA QUILES

ISBN: 978-1-09835-556-2 Print
ISBN: 978-1-09835-557-9 eBook

CONTENTS

Early
Seeds

OUR LOVE

The first time I seen your face I knew it would be true

Because at that moment in time I fell in love with you

I knew that you would be very special to me

I hope that we will be together for eternity

I'm happy to know that you're by my side

As we walk together with our heads held high

I want you to know that you're all I desire

As long as the candle is lit, we'll always have our fire

We fulfill each other's fantasies

And make them into ecstasy

You and I are meant to be

And I always want to feel your body next to me

Our feelings will forever be as beautiful as a dove

And with that symbol, it will remind us of "Our Love"

DAYS

There are days when I want to be alone,
when no one calls me on the phone.
There are days when I want to go somewhere far,
I want to travel to the farthest star.
There are days when I want to lie on the grass,
away from all this trash.
Many talk so much junk
They just don't know that talking will land them in a trunk.
Don't get me wrong I'm not mean, that's just how I seem.
There are days when I want to chill, on top of the highest hill.
There are days when I want to let people know how I feel
I choose to keep it to myself and stay real.
There are days when I want to scream aloud with all my might
I just keep my cool and close my mouth really tight.
All I want is the best life for me
Right now, I just want to climb the highest tree.
There are days when I want to sing the blues
Just a day that I let out all my woes.
I can write poems all day
I have a lot to say
This is how I express my inner feelings,
to all the millions of people who read them.
The more I write, the more my mind expands
My mind is sent into different worlds
At least one trance
Many things inspire me to write that is why I consider myself so bright.

DEATH

Death is a way of life
It may leave people in strife
It will make many people depressed
It may also make them stressed
It's a terrible thing don't get me wrong
But what may help is to sing a song
Many people come and go
But hey, you should just go with the flow
God can't promise anyone another day
So, basically everyone should go their own way
Many people even say that they will die
Many say that they will cry
But really if you think about it
They are off in a better place
Living the good life with God dressed in all lace
So, what you should do is when someone passes away
All you have to do is look up and say
Just wait, I'm coming your way.

I LOVE YOU

I Love you with all my heart

You are my sunshine and I don't ever want us to part

I Love You like a dozen of roses

I love to see all of your beautiful poses

I know that I Love You because you are all I think about

When I don't see your face, I start to pout

You are the person that I want to be with for the rest of my life

I want to always be your loving wife

On that special day when we first met, I knew my life was set

I can write so many things to express how I feel

But prefer to show my actions to prove that I'm real

You are my pride and joy and I want you to be my boy

I remember the first time we kissed, it felt like pure bliss

I only see me and you together

I truly want this love to last forever

You are my King and I'm your Queen

I don't mind if we make a scene

Let's go take a walk on the sand

There I will take your hand and give you a wedding band

I write this poem to let you know that I don't mind telling you how much

I Love You in the snow.

REAL LOVE

Real Love is going through heartaches and pains
It's taking responsibility for all your blames
You never doubt or mistrust that love
Because you and that person should fit like a glove
Whatever mistakes you did in the past
Your feelings and love will always last
You will stay together through thick and thin
Whatever arguments you have
You both always win
You never doubt the way you feel
It will always live as long as the heart you conceal
You hold it deep within yourself
And it always brings you good health.

ROYAL LOVE

It's like rags to riches

A dress with tight stitches

Love conquers All

All who abide by it

No one can make it stay

No one can make it fit

It has Kings and Queens

It never comes out how people seem to talk about it

Love is rich

Love is grand

Everyone is holding each other's hand

Some people will die for it

Some people just don't care

Hey look at me

I have a soft cuddly teddy bear

He is sweet and sexy, and I need him next to me

We have our ups and downs

We very seldom have any frowns

He is an angel sent from above

There is nothing that I can do to describe him except as my "Royal Love"

HEARTACHE

Every day I deny your Love
I push you farther away
Nothing not even your words can make me stay
I don't know why I continue to care
When our love isn't going anywhere
Not even a kiss
Not even a hug
Not even a feeling of bliss from above can make me stay
I'm tired of all the games you play
I'm sorry but I'm through
I can no longer put up with you
It's been sweet, maybe even a real good treat
As I end this, I have one thing to say
Don't ever come back
Go far, far away.

FEAR

Many people have at least one fear
For some it's so obvious, almost clear
It can haunt you night and day
Many people are afraid so it's hard to say
My fear is losing my knowledge
I fear I won't get through college
I keep writing to expand my ideas
And try to conquer my worst fears
Knowledge is the best gift God ever gave me
I'm the only one that holds the key
Now until I get rid of this fear
I will let out a few tears
All I can do is hope and pray
That God will give me a chance to see another day.

MY KING

I have a King
He makes my heart sing
We hope to start a life together
We hope to have our couches in leather
We speak with each other all the time
Not seeing each other would be a crime
Our love for one another is no mystery
If we fall apart it will be considered a catastrophe
I consider him my first love
I put no other man above
My father and God are an exception
I have both of their blessings
I want to marry that man
I truly hope I can
I need him in my life
Only he can take away all my strife.

PRAYER

Lord, I know as long as I have faith
You will always keep me safe
No matter how hard I try
I know with your blessing, I will get by
You are the reason I am on earth
I am the reason my mom gave birth
I'll try to make you proud
On judgement day you'll say aloud
Come home my daughter
I will take you away from the slaughter
You will continue to pray
I will continue to give you another day.

BEAUTY

It is sometimes described as a rose
It may be discovered by doing a pose
It is inside and out
It takes time to experience what it is all about
A lot of people dwell on it
If it is not perfected, they will be considered in a pit
Beauty is a gift from above
It was given to us with a lot of love
So, we should all be thankful
That we have more than a handful of beauty
Beauty is my face
Beauty keeps me in place.

SELF ESTEEM

Help me stay strong and sweet
Help me stay on my feet
Let me be confident within myself
Let me go through the years with good health
Make me wise and grand
Make me lend out a helping hand
Guide me through my life
Guide me to become a loving wife
Love me like I love you
Love me even when I am blue
I will stay close no matter what
I will stay close and be alert
Grant me love and wealth
Grant me a good self
Give me a beautiful family
Give me a smile that will light up the world
So, I can give a trunk of gold.

AFRICA

It is the mother of all mothers
It contains beautiful sisters and brothers
It is one big beautiful land
That no one is scared to take a stand
The people sing aloud, they move, shake, and dance so well
It makes you want to go out to find romance
They contain the most beautiful color that is soft and smooth like butter
Africa is part of me
People may not believe it because of what they see
I hold Africa deep within my heart
With my hopes and dreams for it
We will never part.

ANGEL

Angel of mine
You taste as good as wine
I want you to bless me
I want you to caress me
I love the way you kiss me
You make me feel brand new
Whenever you make me feel this way
I want to get close to you
I love you so much that it makes my heartache
Nothing about you is even fake
All I want to do is please you.

Just Thinking

THE BIG QUESTION

What is Love?

Is it something we have enough of?

Is it something we cherish?

Or, do we let it perish?

Do we know when it is here?

Do we have a clue when it is near?

Will we ever know when we experience it?

I know enough that it does not come in a kit

So, when you find it can you tell me?

How does it make you feel?

Do you feel free?

Does it contain a lot of laughter?

Is it really something to go after?

Or, is it just some fantasy?

That, could never be turned into reality

I do not know you be the judge

Because, what I heard it tastes as good as fudge.

POET

Am I a real poet?

I ask you, how do I show it?

Do I show it in writing?

Do I show it in words?

Do I use certain blurbs?

Am I a good poet?

Do I even know it?

Do I make people's hearts sing?

Do I make their eyes gleam?

Can I make them feel the meanings of the poems that I yell out?

Do I make them jump up and shout?

Do I feel my own words?

Do I send out messages that serves?

Do I make people happy?

Or, do I get the impression that my words are sappy?

Well, I do not know

Till then, I will keep my thoughts on the low.

AM I

Am I appreciative?

Am I sensitive?

Do I take everything to heart?

Am I mean?

Am I cruel?

Do I consider everyone a fool?

Do I love?

Do I care?

Do I spread grace everywhere?

Am I selfish?

Am I spoiled?

Do I consider myself a queen?

What am I?

Who am I?

What am I doing here?

Do I belong?

Do I fit in?

Will I ever have a chance to win?

WILL YOU WAIT FOR ME?

Will you wait for me if I want to leave today and come back later?

Will the distance and absence even really matter?

Will you mind if I find someone else in the meantime?

Just for the time being

Will you wait for me if I take a long trip somewhere to clear my head?

Will you remain alone in our king size bed?

Will you look you at the sky and wonder if I miss you?

Will you wonder if I am still loving only you?

Will you wait for me to show you more attention?

Or, will you just let the neglection continue and never mention

When I tell you that I am going out with friends

when I know you are at home alone

Will you wait for me?

I hear you telling me how much you love and miss me

All I respond is I know, I see

When you wait for my call or text all day

I never meet your expectations, will you wait for me then?

When you clearly tell me what's wrong

When you ask where I've been

Will you really wait for me?

Y & C

Young and confused
What should I do?
Should I find someone new?
Or, should I stay with someone I know is true?
I want to explore
But I am not so sure
I love one person
But I want to get to know another.

Mirror Mirror

MIRROR

As I glanced in the mirror, I seen dark eyes with a dark soul

Trying to feel loved

Trying to feel bold

Eyes with a lot of pain

Pain that sheds tears of blood

A heart that is crushed in the fist and between the fingers of a man

Eyes that have hate for the man who has hurt them

Not wishing for the man to go away

But more that the pain goes away

Life feels so empty without the closeness

of the other eyes gazing into each other

Flames are produced by the scarred eyes

Flames that would cause a fire to the entire world

Real love and Real love only can save these sad young eyes.

AUGUST 15, 1999

The destruction of a young man and his father
The yelling and screaming will only send them farther
They both know they are wrong
Both want to give out an expression that they are strong
The truth comes out from both parts
After this day nothing will mend their broken hearts
A mother full of love tries to mend them back together
But all they can say is goodbye forever
A young woman tries to grow up without fear
But it seems most of the time she sheds a tear
A tear for two men she loves the most
A tear for a brother she might not see again
A tear for a father whom she can still call a friend
All she does is write it down on paper
All she does is hope for the lord to keep them both safer
All she has is the memory of that day
She wishes that everything will be okay
But, in this house it never ends that way.

A YOUNG MAN

A young man dying to be free
A young man saying I hope he loves me
A young man hurt and angry with himself
A young man in decently good health
A young man who made mistakes in his past
A young man who learned from them at last
A young man who is saddened by his ways
A young man who tries to improve it day after day
A young man who struggles to be on his own
A young man who is not alone
A young man who is loved by many
A young man who is worth much more than a penny
A young man who is incredibly special to me
He will always be my favorite friend
From now until eternity.

MASTERMIND

Mastermind with intense love
With all the stars from above
All the trees that move with the air
All the memories that we share
Never again will my heart break
Never again will my heart ache
I know that we will stay
I know each and everyday
My love will be there
And never, will my heart fear.

SILENT CRY

Dear Lord, I have been down this path
Where it is not easy for me to laugh
You know the aches and pains that I endure
Where sometimes I wake up feeling unsure
But, someway, somehow, I see a bright light
I try to believe with all my might
To be certain that the one I'm with is for me
To allow me to set this bottled anger free
I am going through troubled times right now
I feel like the weight of the world is holding me down.

DID YOU

Did you ask me how I am feeling?

Did you ask me about my day?

Did you even notice that I am not feeling well today?

My life feels so empty whenever you go away

Have you even noticed that I am not me today?

Because, I had a nightmare that you were going away

Have you looked into my soul?

Because, if you did you will see a hole

Someone has taken my breath

Someone has stripped me naked and took away all I have owned

My soul, my words, my thoughts, my sounds are all gone

So, today did you ever ask me how I am feeling?

Or, even just how was my day

Did you even notice that I am not feeling well today?

DESPAIR

Did you ever feel so defeated

like you were no longer needed in this world?

Did you ever feel like you could not handle

all the responsibilities that were given to you?

I feel like that right now

My life is so chaotic right now

I do not even have the energy to wipe sweat from my brow

I have so many worries and debts that I feel like giving up

I feel like giving up on this so-called life of mine

I cannot continue to walk around and pretend everything is fine

My heart aches for security

Security in love, family, my career, in health, and home

Right now, I cannot even pay for my cell phone

Why did I quit my job you ask?

Knowing all your credit cards were filled up to the max

I quit because I was unhappy with how things were going

I took a chance and jumped off the cliff without ever knowing

I cry myself to sleep sometimes because I do not know what to do

I feel that I am a disappointment to those who are true

True to me in everyway

Telling me do not worry it will be okay

But when I ask when! I cannot wait anymore!

I am told my dear God will always open another door.

MY STORY

Happiness, new life

Some people are trying to get it right

Lust, butterflies, a clump in my upper side

Giggling, warmth, a feeling of security

You are sure this is the one

The one that makes your heart race faster than a beating drum

Deep hurt

Deep pain

My heart beats faster than a runaway train

No smiles

No joy

No more playing me like a toy

Crying, praying, trying to get my life straight

Knowing when that day comes it will be too late

Remembering, praising, saying everything will be okay

Because, I know tomorrow might be my day

Headache, toothache, a neck pain that will never go away

An anger that boils up inside

My smiles could never hide

A rock in my stomach so sharp as a knife

Cutting through my body ending my precious life.

New
Chapter

IT IS OVER

I am done with you
The love is gone
Go find another
I cannot keep being smothered
I care about you
But I do not want you to be my boo
It has been nice; you know what we had before
But now, it is a total sore
I would rather be friends.

NEW FEELINGS

Damn what is it about you?

Are all your words actually true?

Please tell me you are not playing with my mind

It took me so long to find the one that I want to call mine

You do something to me that I cannot even explain

Your eyes, lips, and fingertips pierce my heart's brain

Damn what is it about you?

Every time I am around you my whole body goes numb

And when you kiss me my body explodes and I …

I want to take us to a whole other level

I want to stimulate your mind with my words

Your body with my lips

And, your soul with my love.

CRUSH

Damn sweetie you make me shiver

Every time I hear your voice

Every time I feel your touch

Yes, we are one under God's sun

I need you

I want you

Because you make me feel so good

As I sit here in my bed writing about you

All I can think about is your smile

and how you always make me happy no matter how bad I feel

I think back to that night on that rock,

you may not have noticed but, you made my day

I do not know if you were serious and I hope you were

But I really care about you

No matter how much I try to get you out of my head

You are always in my dreams when I am asleep in my bed

I want you to marry me

Fuck all these other people around

I need you and you do not need them.

MOONLIGHT

It is like the moon all dark with not much light

It is like a flower in the winter

It does not bloom it withers

No more darkness no more tears

The object has no more fears

No more rain, no more sadness

Not even happiness, just a straight face

One that could never be replaced

The face has no expression, just maybe confused

It maybe even just received some bad news

No more happiness

No more joy

No more playfulness

No more smiles

None of the way the object used to be

It is going to be a whole new tree

From a small seed to a plant

A plant with a new life

One without greed.

MAD

I do not know what to write
All I know is I want to fight
I am so mad, I am so angry
I have so much pain running through my brain
I want to handle it by myself
I will be better off by myself
With no help from anyone
No one at all
All people do is put me down
But I am going to show them
Even if I must go down.

HURT HEART

Hurt Heart no way to mend

No love to send

The way things end, no rules are to be bent

No way to mend

No love to send

A Hurt Heart, an organ apart

No way to mend

No love to send

How much sadness does it contain? Can the heart maintain sanity?

No way to mend

No love to send

So much pain, crying the lord's name in vain

No way to mend

No love to send

It is all your fault, no one else is to blame,

you should hold your head down in shame

No way to mend

No love to send

Way too much hate, no time for a new mate

No way to mend

No love to send

Stay alone in the darkness, do not come out in the sun.

No time for any more fun

Head down in shame, no one to blame

No way to mend, no love to send

CAUGHT IN THE MIX

Sometimes I feel like a page torn in half

Torn between two lovers and I cannot choose a path

My mind is in one place

My heart is in another

There are so many reasons why I want to be with the other

One is about physical attraction

The other is for mind satisfaction

Both bring out the best in me

There is only one I can continue to see

Truth be told, I am caught in the mix

Breaking one of their hearts would be a quick fix

Time is everything and I must not waste

I need to hurry up and increase the pace

My love is like a glass half full

They both have the rope and my throat in a tight pull

I know love is more than skin deep

I do not want them find out

Or, they will put me in a permanent sleep.

STANDING IN THE GAP

I am standing in the shadows of loneliness
This one situation took away all my happiness
I am lying on my back in the midst of ecstasy
Forgetting all about reality
Soft hugs and kisses make me forget
That what lies ahead is the real subject
Bodies tremble and sounds are moaned
Little did I know, I will be standing all alone
I open my eyes and started to remember
We have not used a condom since last December
I felt his liquids rush inside
The look on his face he could not hide
We both knew what had taken place
And that is when the tears started rolling down my face
To my unbelief he did not stay
I cannot believe the man I love would go astray
I thought about the future before I took a nap
And I now realized I am Standing in the Gap.

EMOTIONAL ROLLERCOASTER

My emotions are never stable
With my career, love, and lack of money
Time tells me I will not be able
Able to succeed in this terrible world
Living with a walking liar
Always believing he is higher
Higher than who?
No not me
I am a natural born Queen
The way he speaks
The way he treats me
I cannot wait to leave
I hate the way I feel everyday
Not knowing if the next day we will be okay
This so-called love is like a rollercoaster
Nothing he says to me is ever true
I feel like a nobody to him
He only wants me for one thing
That is to stick it and leave
When it comes time for responsibility
He makes up an excuse that he is not happy.

INTOLERABLE

He looks at me with pure disgust

Then looks at the models and dancers with pure lust

He tells me to dress up in costume so he can be entertained

Not caring if I am going insane

He tells me I am not doing my job as a woman

Obeying his every command

Only when I am summoned

Wow, what kind of position am I letting this so-called man maintain?

I tell you I am about to blow

Blow steam out of my cranium dome

Feeling, crying, sighing while I am still unknown

He wants me to be everything I am not

Wants me to be in every spot

At the same time, I am not superwoman

I am tired of this madness

I need to be blessed.

Fingers Crossed

EIGHTEEN

Eighteen years have passed and at last a new year is here
My heart throbs as I shine my doorknobs for the new me
I look in the mirror and see my reflection
Standing tall like a mature tree
My eyes are happy and sad at the same time
Waiting for my freedom bells to chime
My heart is not the same anymore
It is a new feeling of strength and positivity
It is no way near sore
I am happy to see this day
Hoping that all negativity goes another way
I want this year to be about Independence and rebirth
About new love and moving forth.

LUST

Today was the day my breath was taken away

Your spoken word was an inspiration

that sent an unbelievable sensation through my soul

Your mere presence is therapy to my heart

The pure essence of your love is the best memory to a brand-new start

I want to hold on to this moment for the rest of my life

I want you to bless me, caress me

I love the way you kiss me

You make me feel brand new

I exhaled today

Hoping and wishing you would be all about me

Hoping you feel and notice the same things I see

I want you to enter my world of ecstasy

Where I would make all your fantasies into a reality.

RE-THINKING

Today he told me he loved me
But through his actions I cannot see
I told him we were having a baby
He just looked at me and said oh, really
It was not the excitement I had expected
It was more like I was putting a burden on him
I knew I should have stuck to my guns and made him wear protection
Instead I followed him, and he won the election
I really hate that I put myself in this position.

WARNING

How many times do I really need to warn you that you are slipping?

Where are the flowers, the kisses, the hugs?

When did you stop courting me?

Really, when did you stop loving me?

I need to hear the words I love you come from your lips first

That is something that I yearn for, it is a thirst

Love me

Touch me

Hold me like you used to

Treat me like the diamond I used to be

Make me feel like I am number one

I want to hear you say you are the one Hun

The love making is little to none now

When we do it; it is no longer fun

Are you here with me or somewhere else?

I think you need to stop thinking of only yourself

I understand you are feeling a certain way

about things going on in your life

How do you expect me to still want to become your wife?

Baby, we all go through pain and stress

You forget we have each other and are completely blessed

What do you want from me today?

That is different from what you wanted from me yesterday.

MISERY

The feelings are not as strong anymore
The conversations that we have are a straight bore
I guess our love has faded away
No one has the urge to stay
My curiosity for others is growing strong
Your actions, words, and looks all appear wrong
There is no right way to tell you this
But, being close to you I do not miss
It is not you it is me is what I'll say
I will drop this line on you at the end of May.

Wedded
Unblissfully

THE FIRST DATE

The first date was such a trip
My nerves were out of control and I needed to get a grip
When I saw you for the first time
my emotions began to race out of control
My body trembled with excitement
I had to make sure I was able to hide it
I was unsure how you felt about me
I felt I was not good enough for you
That you may have wanted to flee
However, you stuck around and continued to treat me like a lady
I just kept saying to myself this is crazy
Am I wasting my time?
I was waiting for a sign
All you showed me was courtesy, respect, and a genuine concern
I was so grateful that you were born
I started to believe that you were made just for me
When we were ready to depart
You were all I wanted to continue to see.

THE NIGHT OF

I got home and gave you a call
Just coming from meeting, you at the mall
My heart and mind were ready for the verdict
It was a short pause and you told me what you were feeling
All I was doing was staring into the ceiling
Hoping it was something good you were going to tell me
And it was
You told me that I was the only one you wanted to continue to see
You asked me to become your girlfriend
I of course, accepted the invitation
It was a decision that was not hard to make
Not one thing about you appeared to be fake
Our conversation continued and we got to know each other better
I just knew I had found a true treasure
I was so happy that you chose me and in return I chose you
You reassured me that what you were saying was true
This is going to work because I want it to
I am going to do whatever it takes to make you happy.

MY LOVE NOTE

I appreciate you coming into my life the way you did

I pictured the man you are since I was a kid

I dreamt that I would meet someone like you

That could turn my gray skies blue

You have made me feel so secure in every way

I wish and pray you will always stay

Your personality is flawless, and your intelligence blows me away

Knowing that we can have a fairy tale ending

Makes me excited about our beginning

Your voice sends signals to my brain

I just cannot maintain my composure any longer

You see, I know you were made especially for me

I am blown away that you continue to accept me for me

I want you to know that there will not be another

to replace you in any way

That is why I will not ever be ashamed to say

You are my man.

EXPRESSING

I saw you today and I was elated

I am so glad you took the time out to make it

You make me feel like a queen

You have me so opened you are what I fiend

They say real love takes real time

I am already prepared to get married

Show me where to sign

Your words and actions are genuine

I still get nervous when you are around me

I cannot believe I met your mother

after being your woman for three days

It was such a special moment for me

I was extremely pleased

It felt good being there involved with the special people in your life

I felt so secure and I cannot wait to become your wife

Of course, in due time for that

The thought just ran through my head as I sat

Anyway, I am just telling you how I feel

and letting you know my feelings are truly real.

PROPOSAL

Christmas morning

Jill Scott, he loves me playing in the background

You know that is my favorite song and my heart begins to pound

I step out of bed to head towards the living room

There you are nervous and sweating

That look on your face is not something I will never be forgetting

You had on a blazer in the house to add a bit of flair

At that moment I did not care what I looked like, not worried about a hair

You got on one knee as I sat

I wish I could remember every word you said

But there were so many things rushing though my head

I already knew my answer before you even finished

You opened the box and I could see

all the love and sacrifice you spared on me

I felt so lucky and so blessed

I could not wait to announce to the world,

but my emotions were such a mess

The love we had for each other would stand the test of time

I finally found my life partner

My ride or die.

VOW

You do not have to worry because I am going to hold you down
I will never leave you for a worthless clown
My entire way of being is because of you
We are going to do everything we planned to do
This old news that is trying to resurface has nothing on you
Your actions make me want to stay true
I am so delighted I chose the right path
Knowing that I am with someone who always makes me laugh
You are a real man inside and out
You are all I ever want to talk about
Trust me I am holding this relationship close to my heart
Making sure I always do right so we never part.

WHAT HAPPENED?

Often your past dictates your future society says
Time and time again I beat myself up about the decisions I have made
My thoughts and emotions stab my heart like it is the sharpest of blades
Why do I allow people to make me feel like I am wrong?
I am happy I keep God close
He helps me to remain strong
People look at me like I am the one who just tossed him in the dirt
As if I enjoyed seeing him with all the hurt
They say I just treated him how the men in my past treated me
All I used him for was revenge and to allow my hurt to become free
I feel that he gained more from this relationship than I did
He became a man with me and was no longer a kid
What did I gain but an additional last name?
I do not want the divorce that I am paying for.

ACCEPTANCE

Did I do the right thing by marrying you?
If I would have just waited one more month
would it have really made a difference?
You would have still been stuck in the same rut
I would have still felt the need to take care of your butt
Why do I always feel an obligation to care for a grown ass man?
I need to learn that I am worth so much more than this
I need to make them work harder for my love and kiss
Why do I constantly put my feelings last?
I would have avoided a lot of blues in my past
My heart and body are valuable
I really need to treat it as my temple
Instead of giving every man who gives me attention a sample
Of course, my bad habits cannot be undone overnight
Though I can at least see the upcoming changes in plain sight
Happy will I be when I start truly loving me
So, did I do the right thing by marrying you?
No, because I was not true to myself
So, how could I be true to you, sorry.

REGRETS/GOODBYE

Missing you every day that I turn over on the bed

and you are no longer there

I blink my eyes a few times thinking and hoping

this will make you appear

Do you really miss me or are you saying it

just because it would please me?

I need for you to genuinely love and want me in every way possible

Leaving no doubt in my mind and heart

that we can and will make this work

I know I cannot change the past

or take away the pain or hurt that I caused

I will regret my decision for the rest of my life

I hate that we have lost so much time already

in our marriage because of my foolishness

I want you to know that not one day went by

where I wasn't in the bathroom crying about the mistake, I made

I was so deep into it that I did not know how to stop or even return to you

What would I say?

What could I say?

My love for you runs deep

All I want is for us to stop delaying enjoying our marriage

I have changed

I am softer, I know how to love harder

I will show more affection, be a better wife

My heart is different, my mind and spirit are much more at peace.

At least forgive me even if we do not get back together.

Karma You Dirty Bitch

CONFLICT

He said leave me the fuck alone

I can no longer provide him a happy home

He says I am wrong for not being there

He made himself truly clear

He always blames everything on me

Errors that he makes he just cannot see

Why do I continue to care?

When I know this relationship is not going anywhere

Today should and will be the day

That we will have nothing more to say

He told me that I have nothing to offer

That we should no longer bother and try to mend this broken situation

There is a lot of frustration in me

How could he treat me this way?

TOPSY TURVY

Loving you is an emotional rollercoaster
I try so hard to get the most out of our conversations
When I talk to you it is as if I am pulling teeth
When I hang up, I am left with this empty feeling and grief
You say you love me
You say you adore me
But, in my gut you want to be free
I know you want to leave but
You do not want to hurt me so, you stay
I need you to be real with yourself
If you need to release me go and play
It is okay to go do not stay for me
I refuse to be pitied
I need to get back to me
I need to finally break free
I am scared to let go
Maybe I am the one causing the rollercoaster
I need to realize that it is okay to be alone sometimes in order to heal
This is what I needed to get my mind right
and to become independent again
My life should not revolve around a man except for God and my father
I think this distance was the best for me to see
It is okay for me to be with only me.

SECURITY

All I want is to feel secure

The way things look I will never have more

More than what I have right now which is nothing

I live paycheck to paycheck, and I am sick of it

I am tired of not having any money to my name

My heartache is not a game

Don't you see it? I am going insane!

I am looking for new things to sale

Time and time again I come up short and always fail

I hate asking people for money

I go through the day completely hungry

I only have enough money which will be used for gas

I guess everyone else expects me

to get the rest of the money out from my ass

Damn I am so pissed about my living situation

I make all this money and still cannot find a way to win

I do not think I want to be the strong one anymore

I fucking hate feeling poor.

CRIES

Someone please hear my cries!
I am slowly but surely dying on the inside
I struggle to pay all my bills each month
Damn, this so-called life is fucking tough
I am only 24 and I have no kids
I do not think I want to bring any into this world
My faith, hopes, and aspirations are all turning cold
I have no trust that my life will change
I wish it were like a book where all I needed to do was turn the page
I just cannot shake the feeling of sadness
All the obstacles I endure are pure madness
Everyone tells me everything happens for a reason
The same issues are here season after season
Someone, anyone please hear my cries
Because, I am slowly but surely dying on the inside!

HOPELESS

A miracle needs to happen soon
Please send an angel down to help clean my wound
No one can help me
I am standing on my own two feet
Day after day it feels like one big defeat
It is so sad that I have this feeling of hopelessness.

DARK HOLE

Misery loves company
That is why my face and body are lumpy
Because of the abuse I endure
For a love commitment I was unsure about
All the I love you's and I do's set me back for an eternity
After all the pushing and shoving
there would be something called make-up sex
Where the words baby you will always be with me follow
Time and time again I tried to escape
Telling myself I cannot wait
I am supposed to be a strong woman that stands my ground
But I'm a lost soul that can't be found.

IS THIS LOVE?

Words of hate are spewed each day
Just begging for a reason to try and stay
I wish you loved me more to stay in the fight
Just watching you make plans to take your flight
Once you leave the home will you feel bare?
I hope each day helps me get rid of my fear
Fear of being alone and not good enough
I look around and think
Damn, I need to get rid of a ton of stuff
I want to be protected, respected, and loved
Not yelled at, slapped, and shoved.

REALIZATION

Light skinned, black eyes

Heart break because you lie

I do not want to kiss and tell

I thought I knew you very well

How could you hurt me so?

Why didn't you just let me go?

My heart turned dark with the first punch

Crying and confused all I could do was make lunch

In the kitchen looking out the window smoking a black and mild

Saying to myself damn, I hope I am not pregnant with his child

When he leaves, I am planning my escape

He will probably come home drunk

He always comes in late

How can you say you love me when you play me like a toy?

You leave me at home alone while you are out with your boy

I am sitting home losing a piece of myself everyday

Just to please you in everyway

You think your good looks will always keep me here

Well, I have news for you

I will no longer live in FEAR

Your words mean nothing to me

What I want from now on is Loyalty and Justice for me!

TRYING

I forgave you and you hurt me again
Time and time again I try to be a friend
I try to understand you may have had a rough past
So, I just need to stay strong for us to make it last
Cursing, screaming, and fighting every night
I cannot seem to find happiness it is nowhere in sight.

EMPTY

So many years
I tasted salt from my tears
Trying to bury all my fears
The soft kisses and tender hugs
can never take back the memory of nights spent laying on the rug
Laying on the rug because I no longer had the energy to stand
Stand up for my rights to be loved and adored
Hearing from your own lips that I made you bored
All the money spent cannot pay for your love
The divorce papers you never had the courage to serve
My heart is cold, my feelings are numb
Fake laughs, fake you, faking every word you spoke
Everything I gave up
I am the one looking like the joke!

SORROW

Broken promises

Empty heart

I should have known and seen the outcome from the start

Empty kisses, empty bed why did I allow you to get in my head?

Through all the struggles and all the pain

I look at the mirror

My face displays the strain

The reflection that I see

No longer looks like the person I used to be

The tears keep flowing at random times

I feel like the past six years were filled with lies

You say I started the ending of it all

But the reflection in your eyes says you are enjoying the fall

What we built can no longer be

I need to begin the journey of loving me.

THE ENEMY

Sleeping with the enemy
He's blinded to the pain he causes me
Feeling uneasy and restless
Looking up at the ceiling feeling helpless
So many thoughts running through my head
Each night it's hard to fall asleep in the bed
The emptiness in my heart grows more each day
He makes constant excuses on why he needs to stay
Truth be told I cannot wait to be free
My mind, heart, and soul are screaming for clarity
Waiting to be able to clear this negative energy in my home
Ready to go into hermit mode, wanting to be alone
Needing to heal this inner wound
The toxic thoughts I can no longer consume

GOODBYE LOVE

The end is near

I am manifesting something new for my life my dear

I have grown to understand the meaning of it all

Knowing my worth is more important to me

This will prevent another fall

You will not make the move so I must

The words spoken from your lips I can no longer trust

I am trying to break free from this bond cordially

Attempting another outcome from what happens normally

I wish you nothing but the best on your new endeavor

The ball and chains we must immediately sever

I want to walk a new path

I have already done the calculations, it is simple math

Two plus two equals goodbye

We are no longer seeing things eye to eye

Please make this easy and just pack your things and leave

I just want a clean break

I promise I have nothing else up my sleeve

Thank you for the lessons you taught me throughout the years

You provided me the tools and knowledge to move forward with no fears.

WHAT I'M LOOKING FOR IN A MAN

Someone who is supportive of me
Someone who is loving and respectful
Someone who is loyal and honest
Someone who is beautiful inside and out
Someone who is funny
Someone who only wants me
Someone who knows I can take care of myself
but wants to take care of me anyway
Someone who wants and loves children
Someone who is a provider
Someone who is ready to be a father
Someone who is ready to be a husband
Someone who wants to be a friend
Someone who has already disposed of their old garbage
Someone who values my opinion and who values me
Someone who values and loves my family
Someone who values and loves his family
Someone who is motivated and driven
Someone who surprises me just because
Someone who expresses love for me every chance he gets
Someone who cooks and cleans
Someone who loves himself
Someone who respects women
Someone spiritually in tuned

Looking
Forward

MANIFESTING

Manifesting a new destiny
Seeing my future more clearly
Ready to claim the positive things for me
Praying all the negativity away
Taking my life more seriously, I will no longer play
Taking this precious time to focus on me
Re-evaluating my mistakes, the ones I ignored to see
Growing each day differently than the past
Making sure this time the love for myself, is what lasts
No more dwelling on the what ifs and what nots
No more drowning my sorrows with fireball shots
Focusing on rebuilding my self esteem
So, I can really recognize the true person
who wants to be a part of my team
No more tears wasted for those who did not understand
Understand the true meaning of being a real man
It is not my fault their mothers failed them
It is not my fault they were too broken to recognize a gem
I am manifesting a new destiny
Seeing my future more clearly
Ready to claim the positive things for me.

CONTENTMENT

I release any energy that no longer serves a purpose

Keeping my mind clear, trying to stay focused

Self-love and self-care

Prevented those in any capacity to treat me unfair

Loving me and keeping the faith

Never giving up

Keeping my heart safe

I am still open to love but I am focusing on me

Happiness and good health are the key

Finding balance and inner peace

Looking forward to the blessings that I know will increase

Living my best life healing and praying

The work on myself is something I will be slaying

Releasing the negativity that has held me down for so long

Forgiving myself for what I have done wrong.

NOTE TO MY UNBORN CHILD

My little unicorn I cannot wait to hold you in my arms
Mommy is working on herself so you will be born without harm
I know you have tried to come in my life before
When the angels took you back
The pain I felt I could not endure
Knowing you have always been there in spirit rooting for me
Helps motivate me even more because it is you, I need to see
You my little angel will help me heal
The love I already have for you is a very big deal
I did name you once before my star
I feel your spirit everywhere even though you are far
When you decide to try again to come back in my life
You will be the biggest blessing I'll ever receive,
and you'll take away the strife
Mommy loves you so much my dear your happiness is long overdue
You, I know will be a sacred love, the love I know is true
You will be gifted and creative just like mom and dad
You will be the best gift we will ever have.

TO MY FUTURE HUSBAND

I am preparing myself for you
Cleansing my mind, body, and soul for you
Dreaming about the way you will feel
Your touch, your lips, your fingertips, my heart you will steal
I am excited about your mind
I can picture us walking through the park with our fingers intertwined
Your eyes are so seductive, your smile is so pure
My body will vibrate from your touch, you are the magic cure
We will take our time to make sure this is right
Once we pass the awkward phase neither will want to take flight
We will respect each other's needs and wants
You will probably bring new culture and make us some croissants
This bond we will develop no person can break
The love we show each other will aid in the children we will make
Our family foundation will be solid, I can see this clear as day
Being partners during the serious times and always leaving room for play
You will be unique because I am looking for something brand new
We will be proud of the home we have built, the love that we grew
We will sit on the sofa staring into each other's eyes
Planting sweet kisses every chance we get
We will be grateful for all the time that is spent.